Seabird
Damian Bird

Published by Life Force magazine Books. Devon, England. 2017.
www.lifeforcemagazine.com

Photographer: Damian Bird. www.damianbirdphotography.com
Editors: Damian Bird and Alice Bird.
Designer: Alice Bird.
Words: Fishermen's own. Edited and arranged by Alice Bird.
Printed in Devon, England.

This book is for my son, Ethan.

All rights reserved. No part of this publication may be reproduced or transmitted in any form or by any means electronic or mechanical, including photocopy, recording or any other information storage and retrieval system, without prior permission in writing from the publisher. All photographs : © Damian Bird 2017.

With enormous and heartfelt thanks to:
Christabel and Francis Ames-Lewis, Marion and David Moth and all of our other sponsors, without whom this book would never have come into being.
My wife Alice for all her efforts and my children: Ethan, Thea, Hermione and Florence for putting up with their parents working all the time.
But most of all to the community of fishermen in West Bay, Bridport, Dorset: David Sales, Peter Newton, Mark Cornwell, Aubrey Banfield, Donald Johnson, Ted Hook, Jamie Smith, John Worswick, Jack Woolmington, Stephen Elsworth, Nick Rich, Danny Burden, Lenny Follett, Jez Greenwood and Shane Flynn.

ISBN 978-1-9998602-0-2

Peter Newton and Jack Woolmington

Cuttlefishing, Crabbing and Lobster Potting

Peter Newton: I was an angler when I was a kid. I always liked the sea and I started fishing, I suppose, because I didn't want to go to work! I started fishing for a living when I was about 18, in 1973. That was in Essex. I'd always come down here to West Bay on holiday. I had friends down here and it was just a natural progression to move here. I mean Essex was all right and the eel fishing was good, but basically you're fishing in rivers and estuaries and it was nicer down here.

None of my close family have ever had anything to do with the sea. My Dad can't even get onto a boat without feeling sea sick and I was born 60 miles from the coast. Recently, though, my Great Aunt did the family tree, on my Dad's Mum's side. The only connection she found with the sea was a Captain John Brewster who was a Privateer for the East India Company. So I suppose, I am related to a pirate. He was a famous one too because he had this church built and dedicated to him in Norfolk and his tomb is still there. My Great Aunt saw it before she died. I can't remember what year he died in, but apparently they had a stately home in the 17 or 1800s. They must have lost all their money before I turned up.

Fishing is one of the most dangerous jobs that you can do. You're always learning. You're never going to learn everything though, otherwise it would be too easy wouldn't it? The trouble with fishing is, like with anything, familiarity breeds contempt. You truck on, truck on and truck on and then something out of the ordinary happens and you think, bloody hell that was close. You've got to watch yourself. Self-preservation is a great thing. Always respect the sea. Never be complacent.

I couldn't imagine doing anything else. Well, I've never done anything else really. I've only ever had a proper job for six months. I also used to shoe horses a bit but then again, horses are another love of mine so that was more of a hobby than work too. I like working on my own. I have the odd conversation with the seagulls, cuss the boat, cuss myself. Some people don't like it at all, but it doesn't worry me whatsoever.

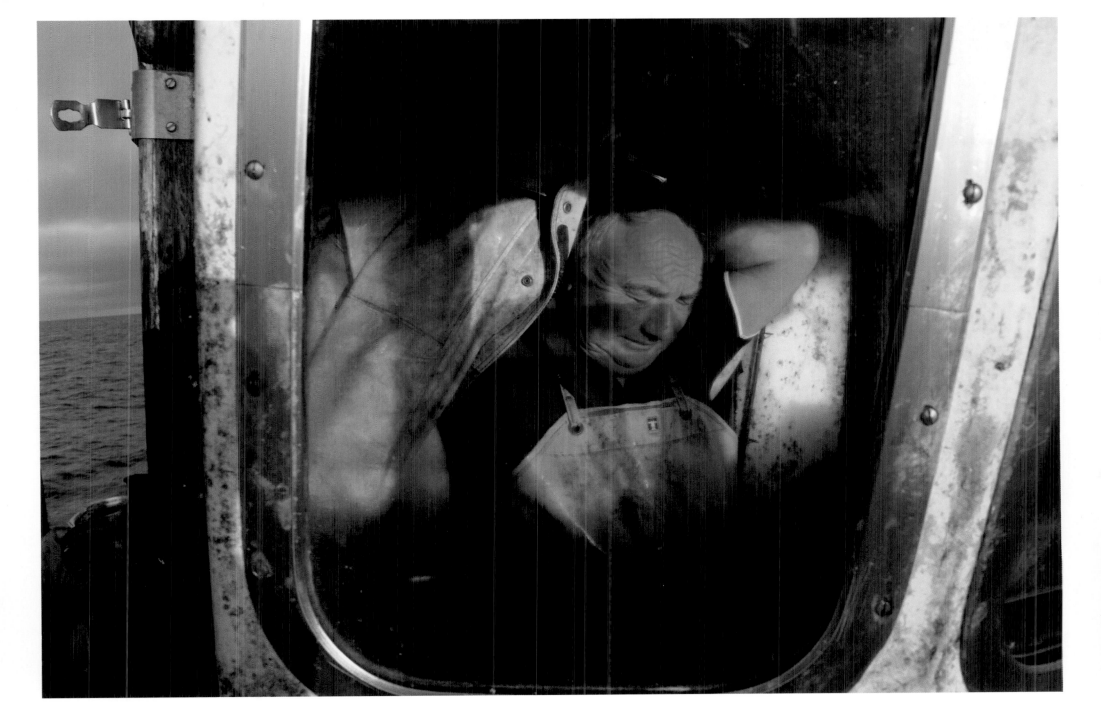

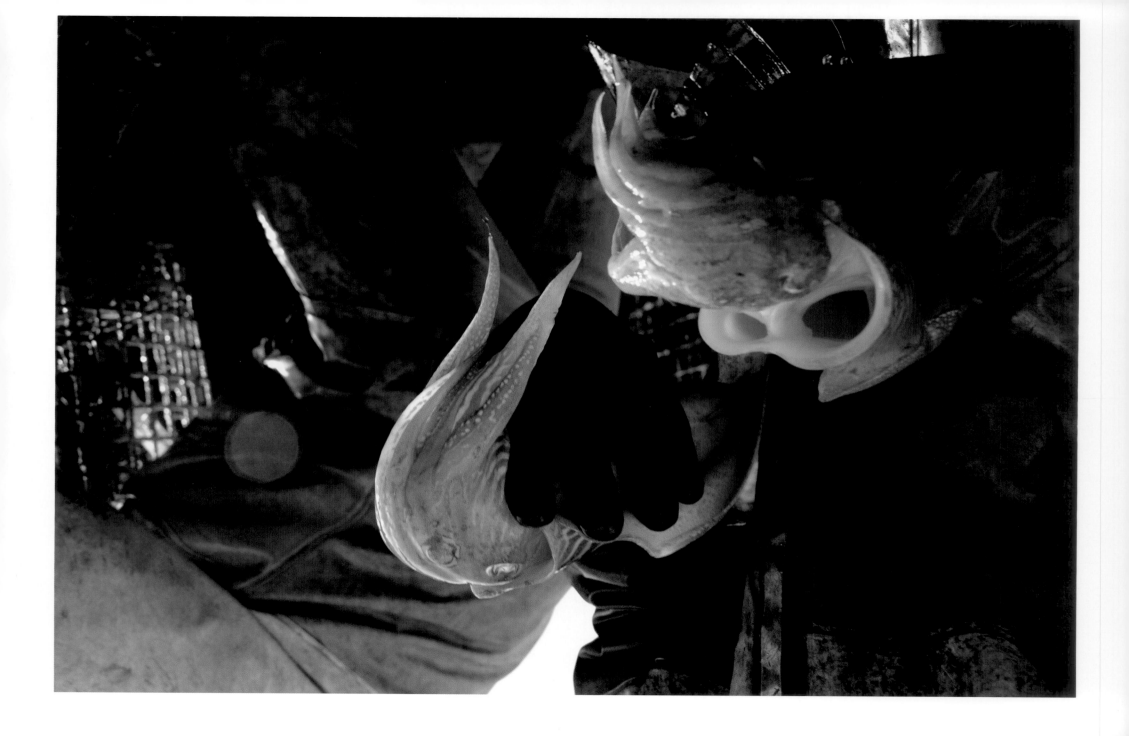

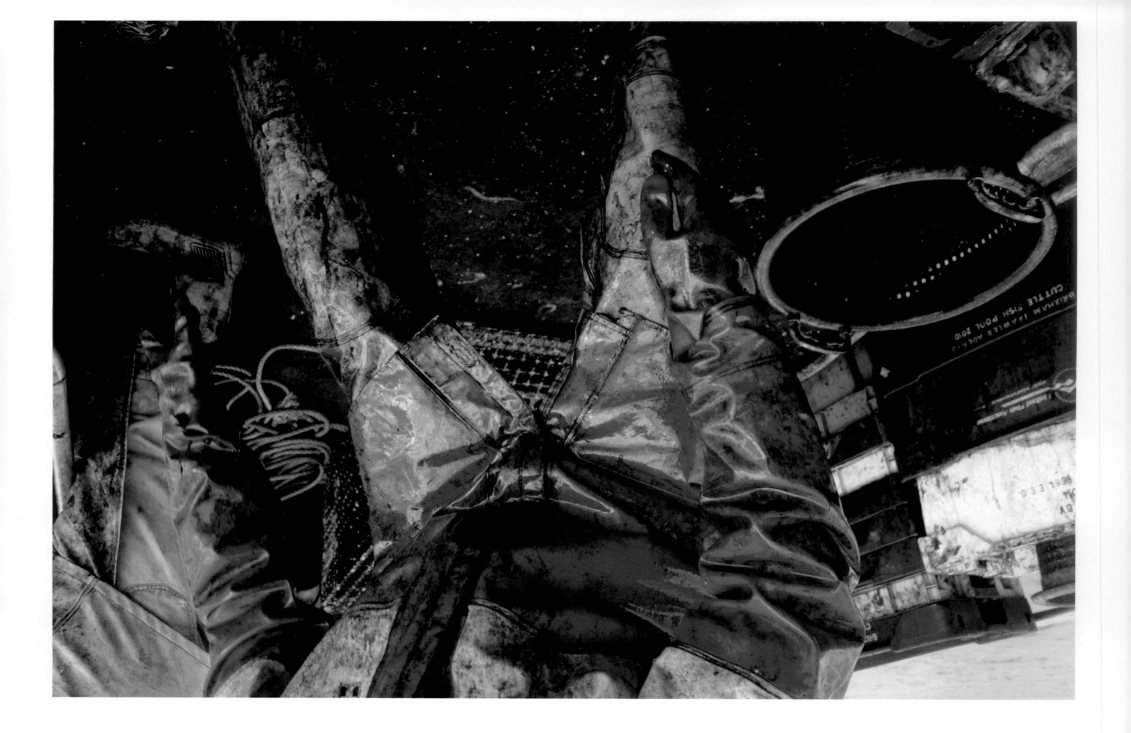

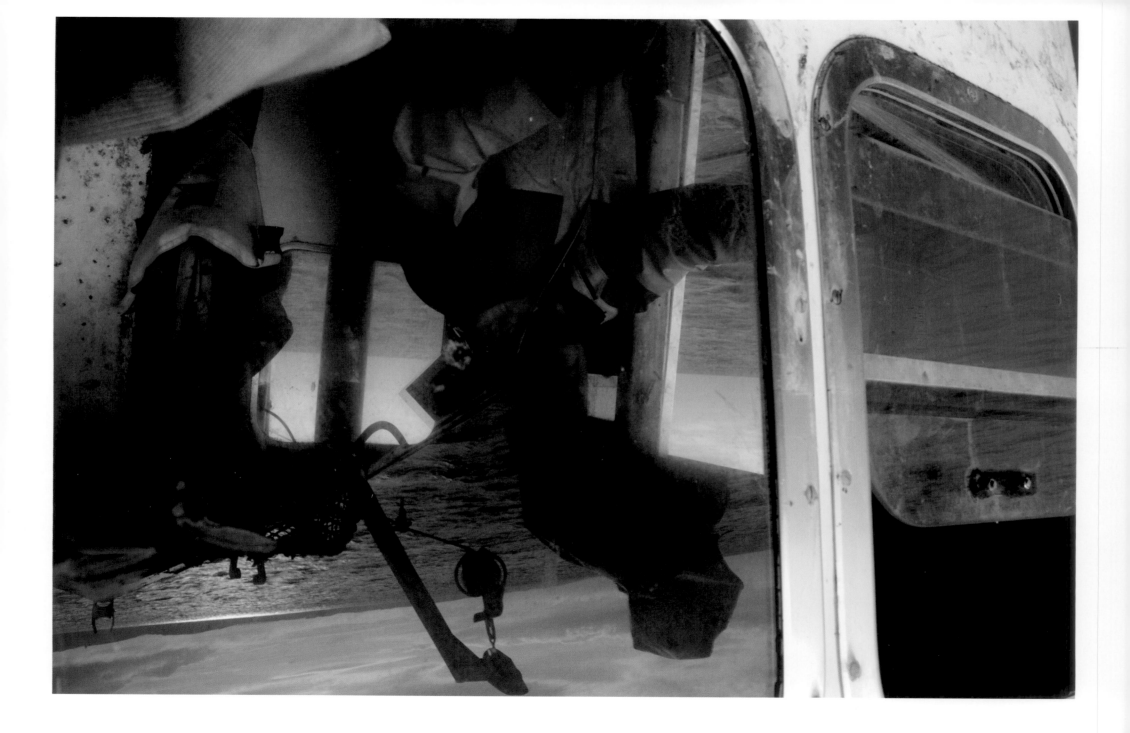

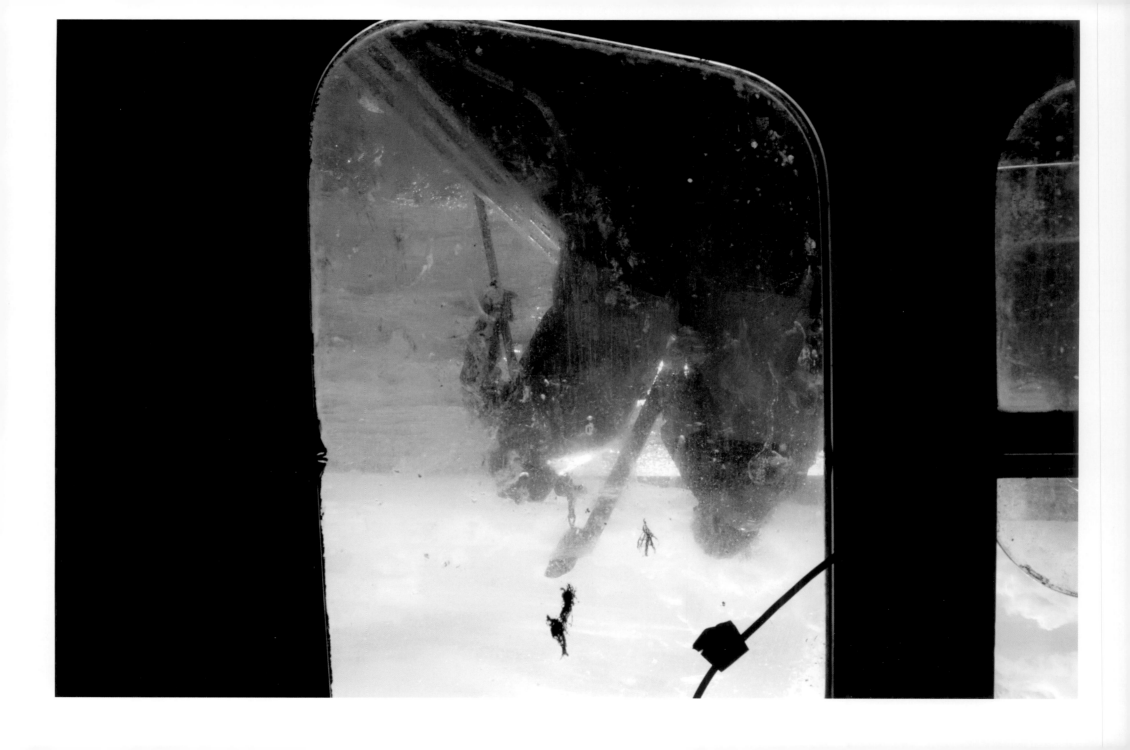

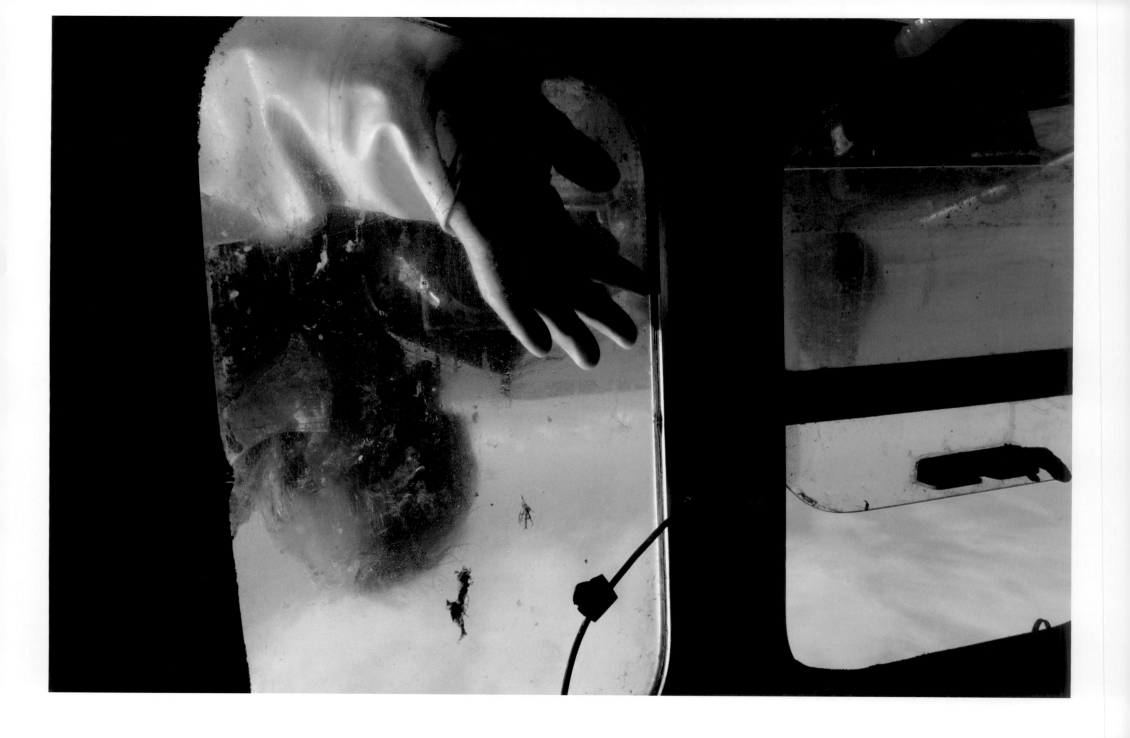

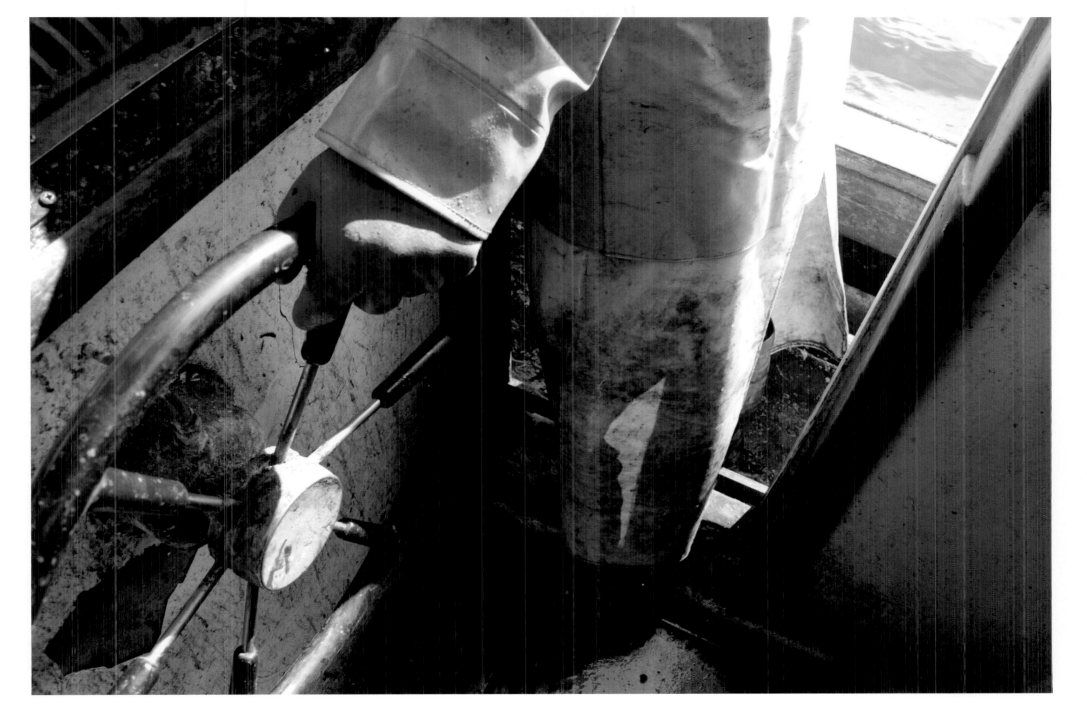

Jack Woolmington: I started fishing in 1960. Prior to that, when I was a kid, we used to catch mackerel off the beach with nets, so I've always been involved with it. My dad had fishing boats in the harbour before I did. I grew up with it. Originally I went out catching eels in my early 20s. Fresh water eels. And I managed to save enough money, over a four year period, to buy my first boat. I went straight in with a 30-foot boat because I knew what you needed in West Bay. I fished for most of my life, but then the boat was getting older and I was getting older, so it was time to stop. Now I work for Pete for just two months of the year. I enjoy it because it gives me a break from the factory. I like to get my injection of salt and I get paid for it as well.

David Sales

Crab and Lobster Potting

David Sales: My cousin Bill led me into fishing when I was 17. We talked about having a boat, because we'd always been on the sea as nippers. I was working on a farm at the time and I thought, if I'm going to go fishing I've got to get some experience. So I went to Swanage and met up with this fisherman, Maurice Lane, who was quite a character and he said, "Yes you can come over for the summer", which I did.

That summer, Maurice's partner broke his leg. He had Polio. So I stayed all the winter and then I ended up staying two years with him. He was a hard character and he had no fear of the sea whatsoever. He was a good teacher and when it came to having a boat of our own and applying for a grant, my cousin Bill's people put the money in but I put the experience in and we had a boat built down at Appledore. We started by catching lobster and crab. We did quite well but the trouble was, Bill didn't want to work. It got to the stage when I had a couple of kids, well at least one, and I had to work. So when I had the opportunity to buy the boat off Bill, I took it.

I used to make my own lobster pots out of wire and buy hoops that the French used to make barrels with. Matt Harvey, down at Newlyn, used to import them, because he dealt with the French a lot. In those days, and it's the one remarkable difference between those days and now, we were still using natural materials. The ropes were manila and sisal and because they were all natural, they used to rot. We used to have them tarred and dip them in Cuprinol and all the rest of it, but you couldn't fish like we are today, in the winter. Then synthetic ropes started to come out and that was a revolution, not only here, but around the World because they didn't rot and they were 10 times stronger.

There weren't the markets there are today. When I was fishing with Maurice we used to take our lobsters up to Southampton to a pub called the Rising Sun and for the cruise-liner trade. The lobster fishing around the coasts of Britain was a cottage industry, done in the summer time. That's when the visitors wanted lobster in the pub. In the winter, there wasn't any lobster because you couldn't do it. The gear wouldn't do it. It wouldn't stand the winter gales.

David Sales: When my wife and I were about 43, we found a house in the Western Gazette and moved to West Bay. We wanted a change. I'd got fed up with big boat crew problems and the tides up in Studland used to drive me nutty.

I didn't really intend to go fishing again and the lot down here were terribly old-fashioned, they really were. We were doing this and that, but there wasn't enough work to keep us going. And then I looked down at West Bay and thought, I reckon there's a lobster to be caught off here and we bought a boat in Penzance and we towed it home. Sea Dragon it was called. It's still about. We see her often when we're in Newlyn. I did really well and so I had my boat the Gillian S built. My wife Gill opened up a fish restaurant in our barn. I caught the fish and Gill sold it.

When I first started at West Bay, I didn't have a clue where the ground was. I put some pots down and my pal from Swanage came with me to haul them and I think we had 10 or 15 lobsters. He said, "You haven't made a bad mistake here, have you?" I put some pots out two or three miles on what we call, The Big Ledge. I was out there, one fine day, all at peace with the world and I had three strings of pots there, when I saw these big boats coming over the horizon and I thought, "What's going on here then?" And it was 16 of these big Brixham scallopers. And the bastards went right through my gear. I got in front of one of them with a floating rope and steadied him up for an hour and from then on, I was at war with scallopers. Fortunately, I was on the Sea Fisheries Committee who controlled the waters at the time. And in this particular area, which goes as far as Lyme Regis, we got the new 12 metre bylaw in place which excluded boats of more than 15 metres. So we got the scallopers kicked out which left us with some 12 metre boats, which weren't really much of a problem at that time. So I had a few years fishing up here, quite peaceful. You used to get a bit of trawling activity up East, but if you didn't put your pots in a daft place, you didn't get trawled up. Then all of a sudden scallops started booming and the big boats started creeping in again. They didn't give a damn or care and they were just about getting up everybody's nose. I always remember, just out here, there were eight of them here one week, up and down, up and down. Scratching the ground all to pieces.

We put together a bit of a dossier; photographs and what not and went to No.10 with them. We showed them the gear. We showed them the damage the scallopers had done. Well, three months later we had our ring protected area. It was about 60 square miles from Beer, down through to just off Burton Bradstock. Then we managed to get an extension right the way from Burton Bradstock to Abbotsbury, which was another 30 square miles. Ever since, the fishing has slowly picked up within the marine protected area. We are all small boats and it's working very well. Donald, does a lot of netting. Pete does potting and they do the cuttlefish in the spring. Each does things his own way. We're not big enough to interfere with one another. We're a good community. We all help one another out when we can. That's how it should be.

Mark Cornwell

Trawling

Mark Cornwell: I started working with my dad after school and at weekends when I was 14, potting and netting. I left school and went dive chartering and then to college to learn mechanics. But I wanted to come back here and when I could afford it, I bought my own boat and went back to fishing for a hassle-free life. I like the early mornings. It's a peaceful time. I don't think I could afford to go fishing if I couldn't fix the boat myself. I'm pretty au fait with everything on the boat. I fit everything and fix everything. My father was always super mechanically minded, so I was brought up repairing things.

The fishing community, in general, is brilliant. It's like a big family. I know people from Cornwall to Scotland. It's a very small world. Everybody knows exactly what everybody else is doing. There are plenty of guarded secrets of course, but we've been helped out, big style, by lots of people. Although they like to make out they won't help you, we do get helped out quite a lot. Any information I've needed is out there. I think, once you're accepted, you're all right. It's a club.

The longest trips we do with this boat are 36 hours, but we don't tend to do that unless we're fishing a long way off. Fuel costs are considerable. Years gone by, fuel wouldn't have been in the equation, whereas now, it's our biggest expense. It's red diesel. We burn 2000 litres every week. We generally work six days a week. We try to have Sundays off, but sometimes it can be a bit more than that. It all depends on the weather. If you've been tied up for a week or more, then you have to do a bit more to catch up.

Trawling can be dangerous. Anything and everything can go wrong. Engine failure. Pipes, wires that could break. Blocks that could snap. The weight is colossal. You have to keep on top of it all to make it as safe as it can be. I wouldn't say we make a hugely successful career out of it, but I have a lovely way of life. I don't want for much and I think I've got the work-life balance pretty sussed at the moment. Gone are the days when you can go hell for leather and catch whatever you like and land it. That's not going to happen anymore, so you've got to get that into your head. I don't want to fish like that anyway. I would rather it was sustainable, worth more and we had to catch less of it.

We fish next to the protected area which is closed to all forms of towed gear. I think the protected area has had the effect of concentrating a lot more boats into a small area, which has probably had a bigger impact on the ground that's not protected. The fishing has been displaced out of some areas and into other areas and also people have moved into other things like whelking which is not affected by quotas and not at all policed in this area. But sometimes fishermen can be their own worst enemies. Everything should be managed and policed and if the balance is right then we can all have a good future. I'm quite looking forward to it!

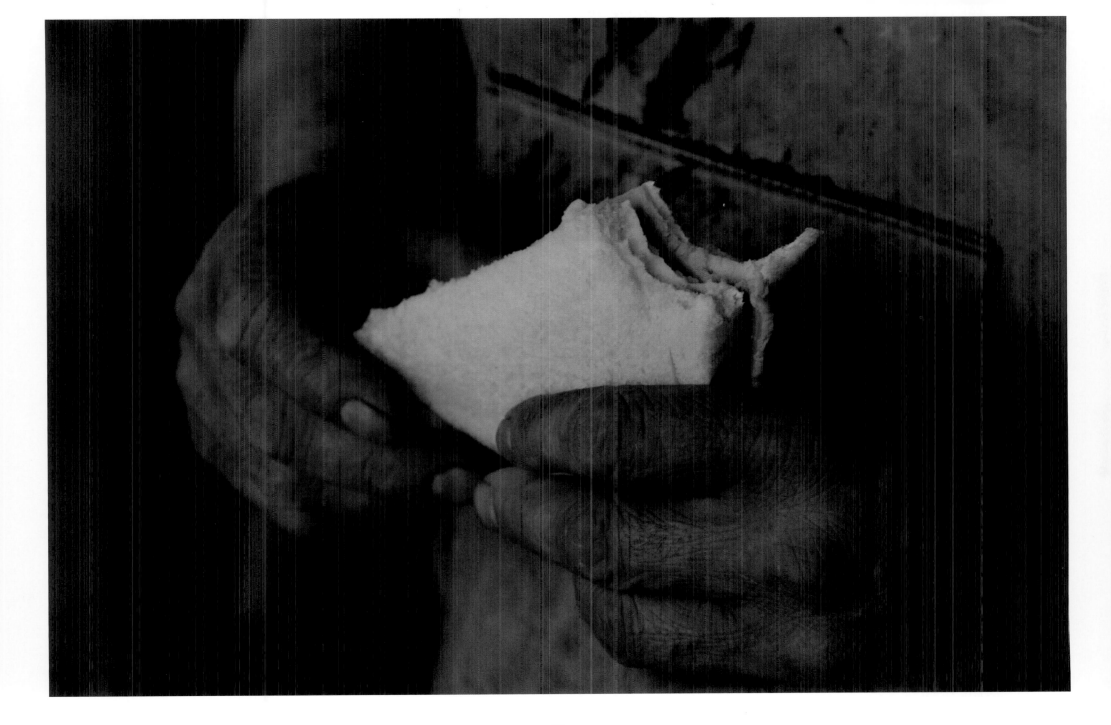

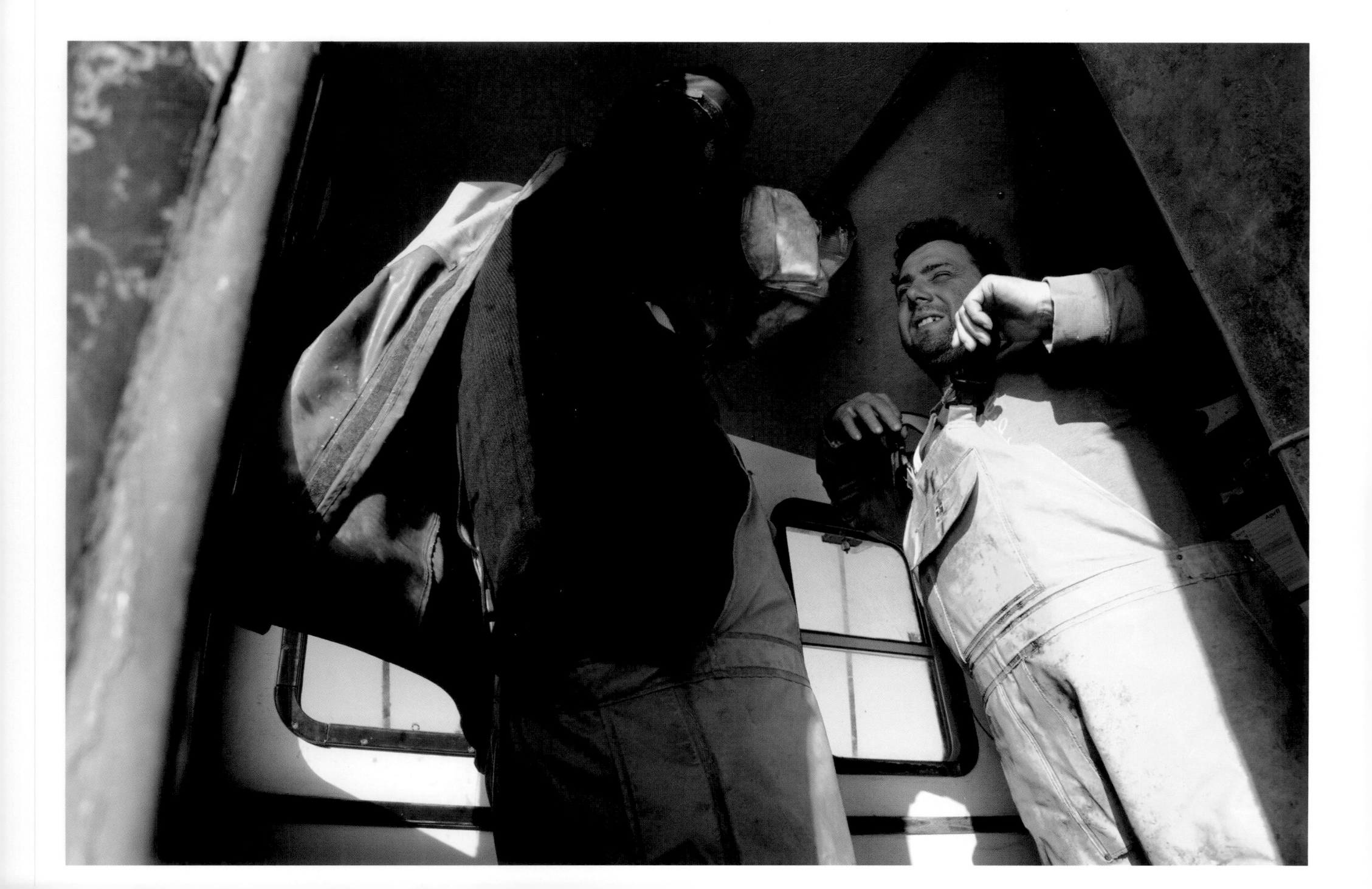

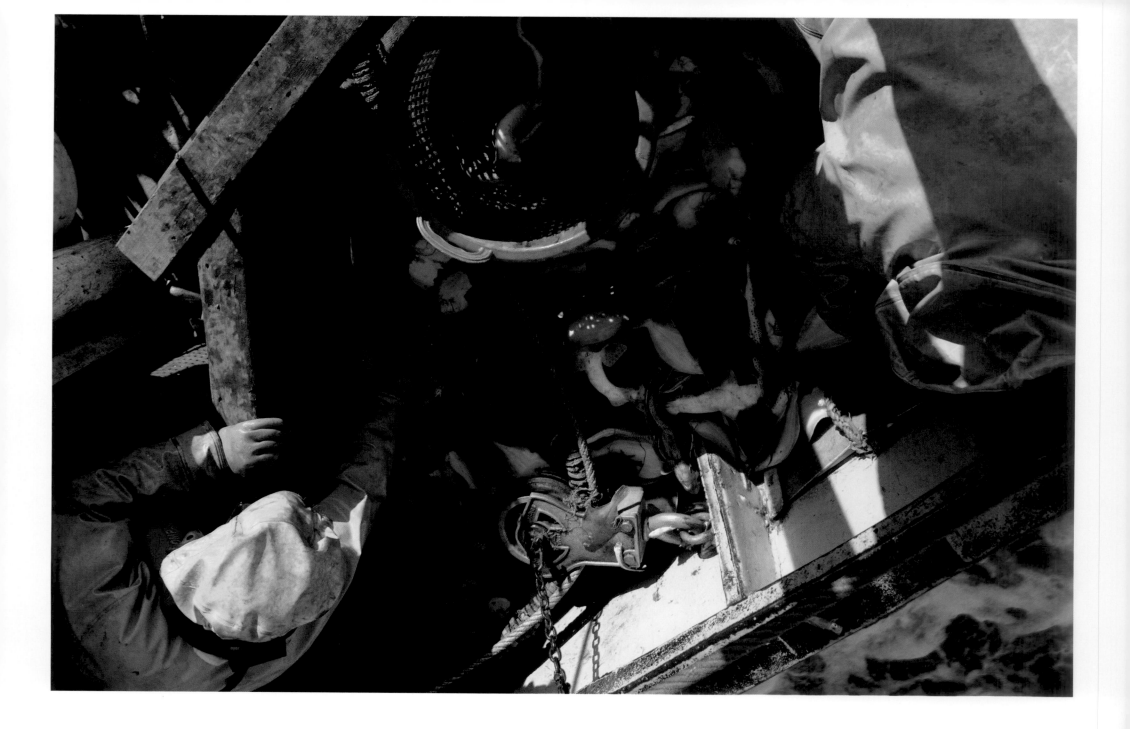

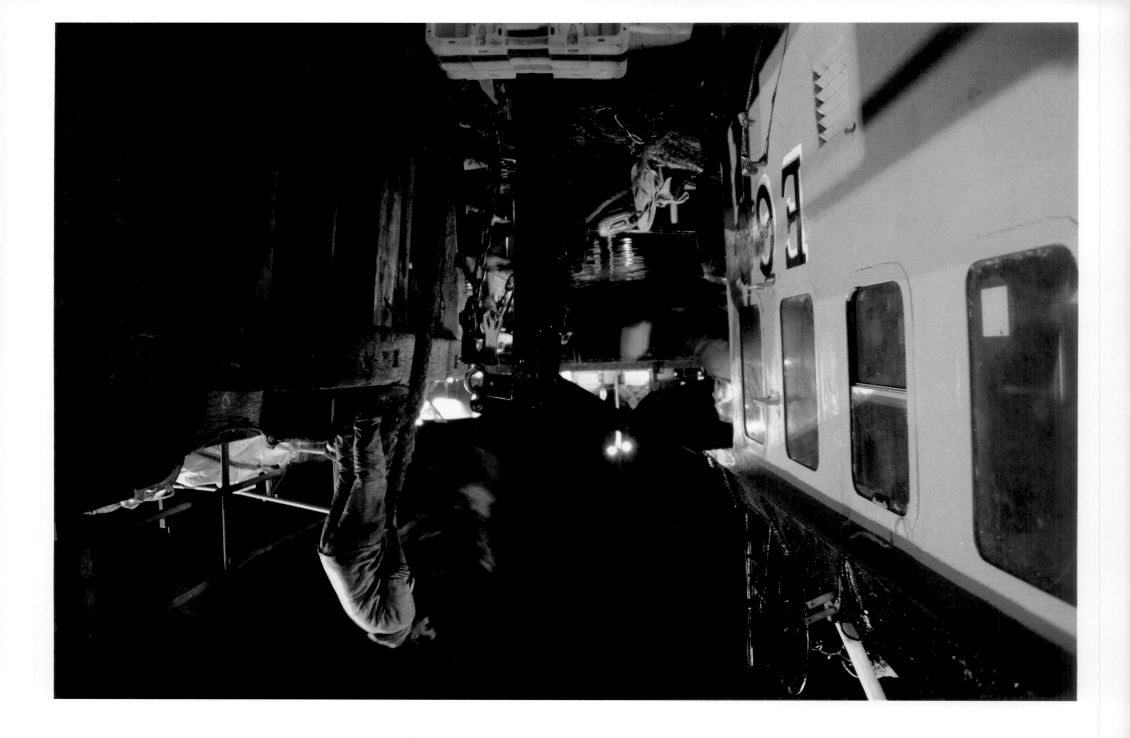

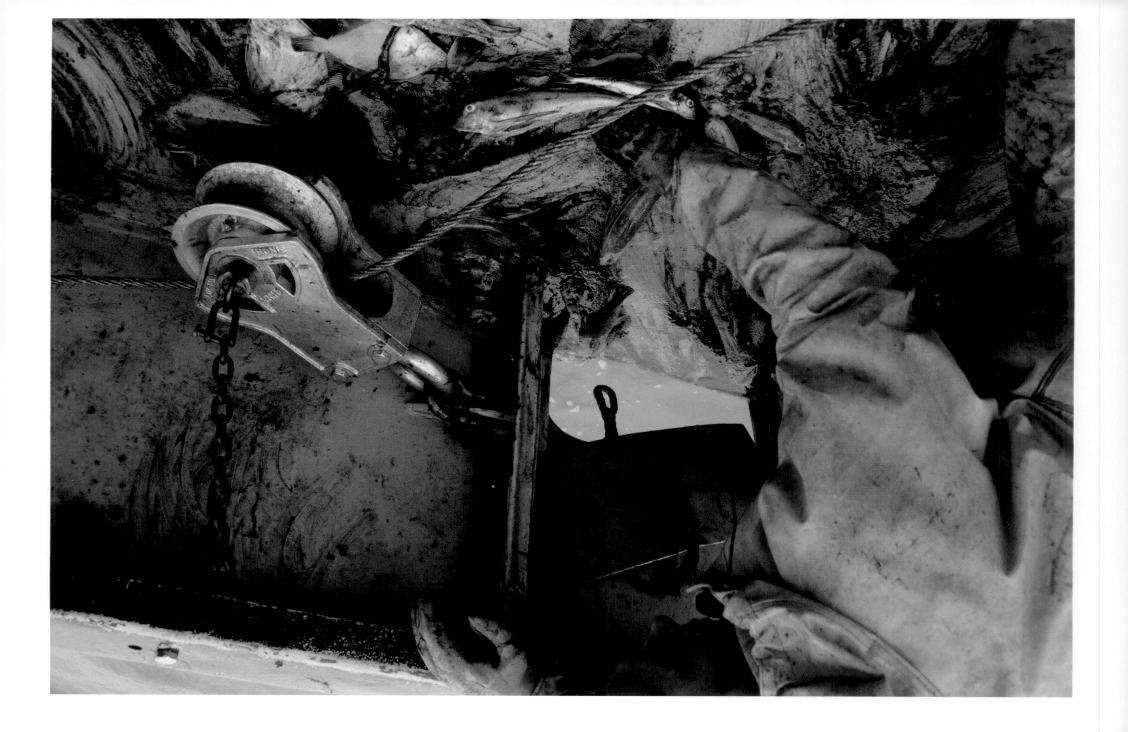

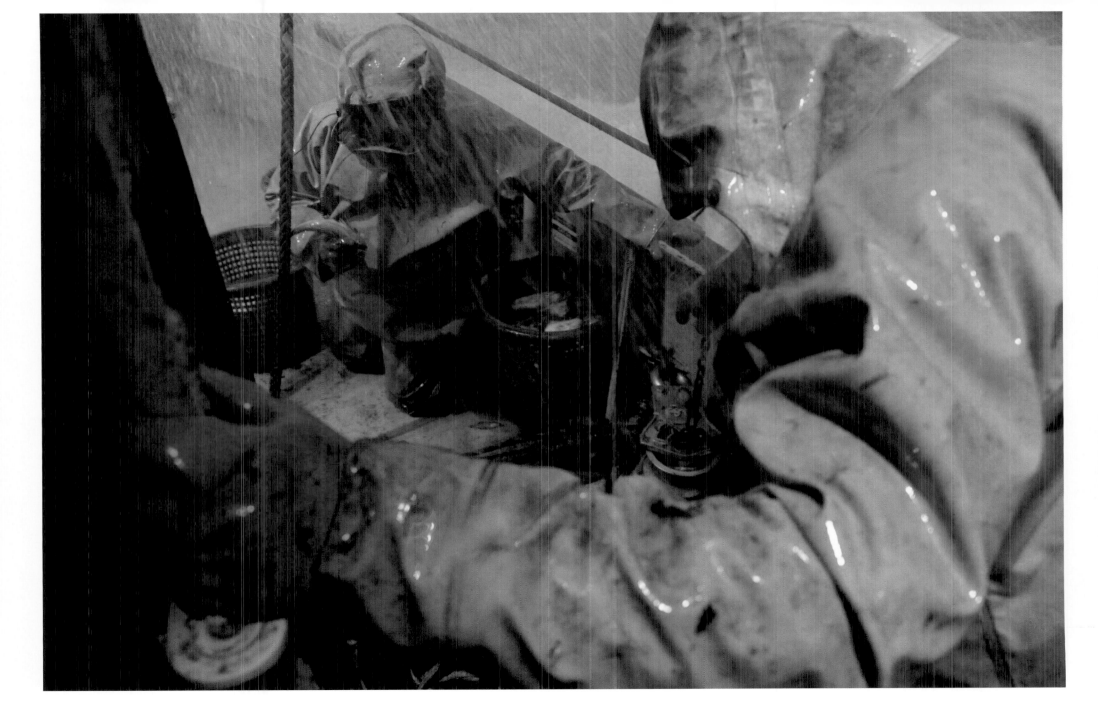

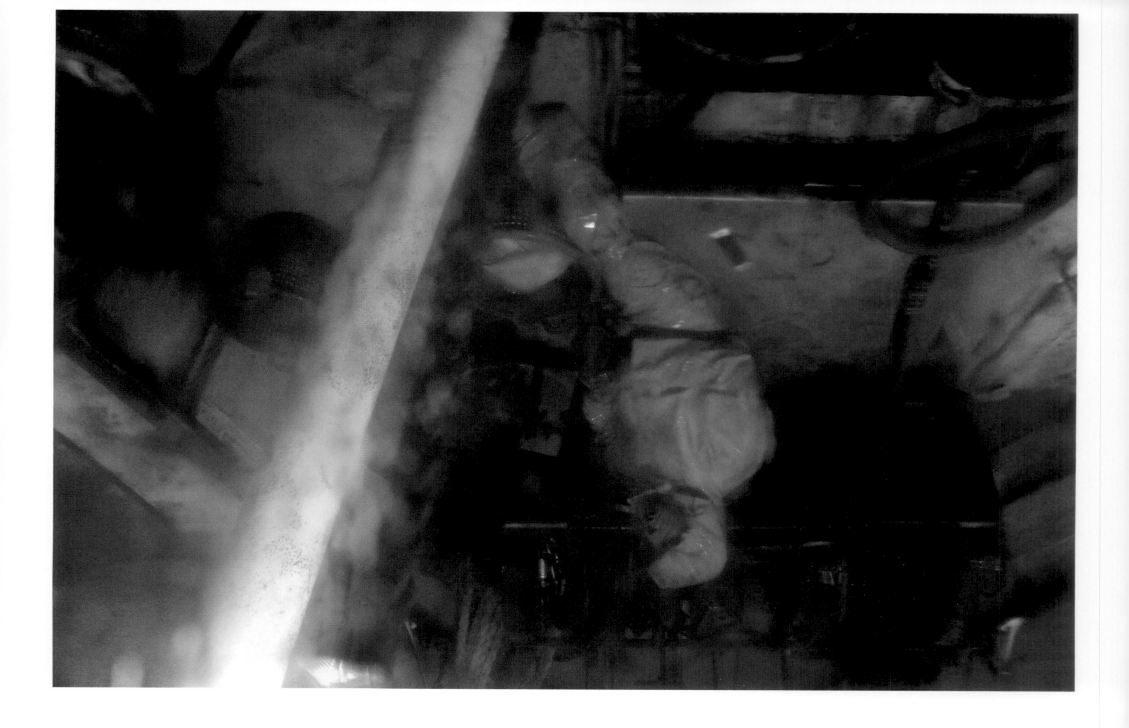

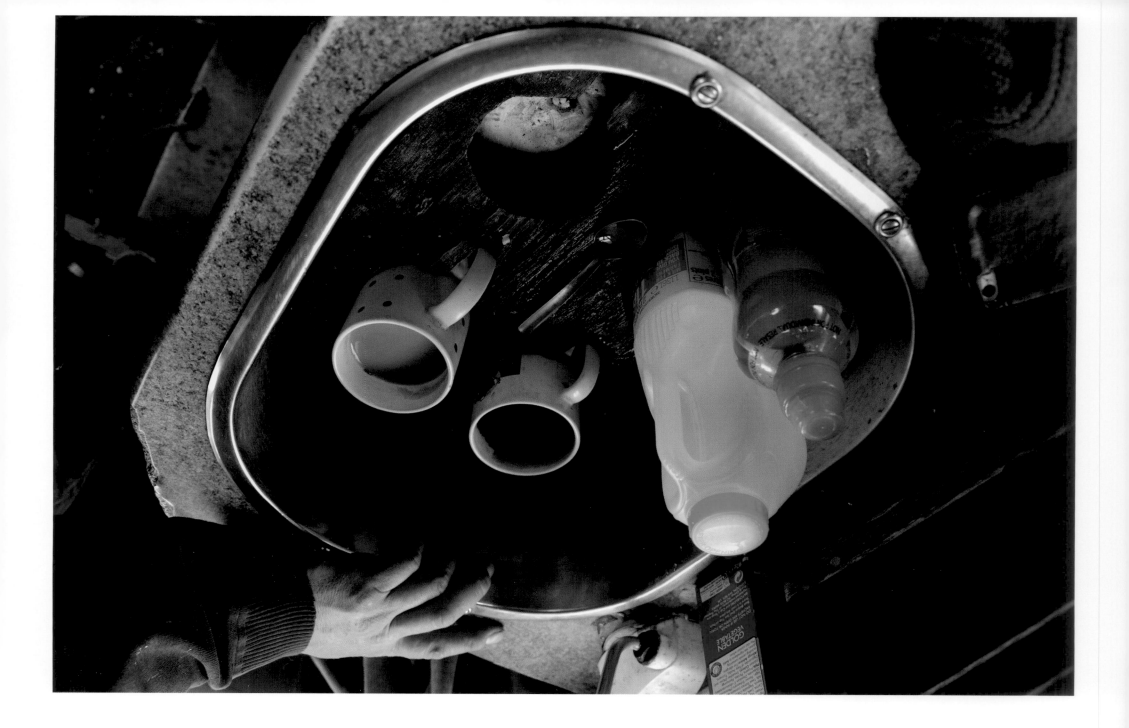

Donald Johnson

Netting, Crab and Lobster Potting

Donald Johnson: I've always fished as a hobby but I went commercial about 25 years ago when I developed a bad back. I just built my boat, and went fishing.

I originally had the boat built for netting, but I mostly have to go potting now because we're not allowed to catch the fish anymore because of quotas. I like getting a good catch, although, perversely, if you continually get good catches, it becomes boring then. Same with life, isn't it? If it becomes easy all the time, it becomes boring doesn't it?

I mostly catch sole, ray and plaice. We used to have sporadic bass fish and mackerel was abundant at one time too, but that's all coming to an end now. The fish are moving. Bass stocks are moving up to the North Sea. But because the dredging's stopped here, it's helping to increase the local fish and shellfish stocks in general, which is all good for the marine environment.

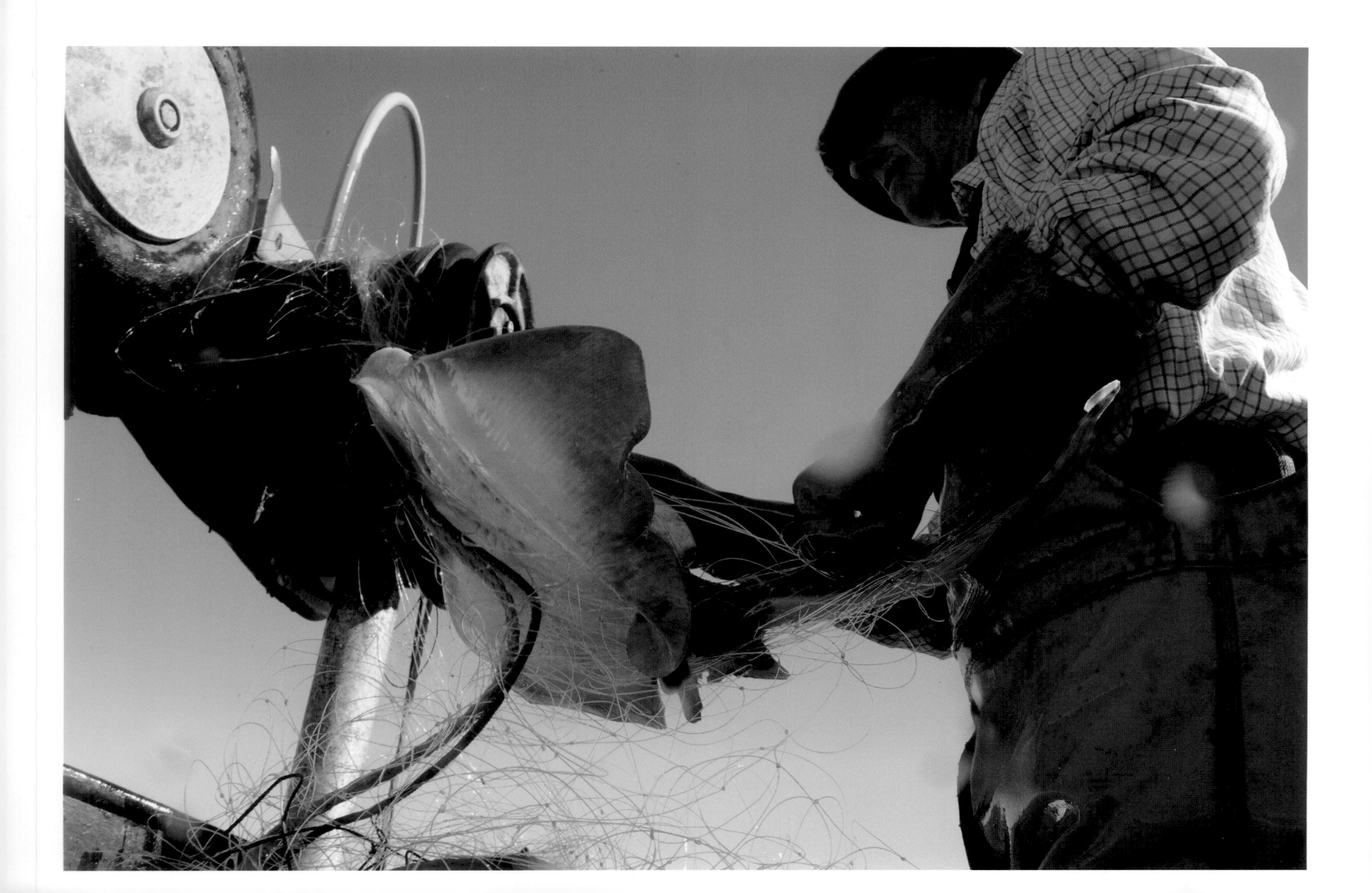

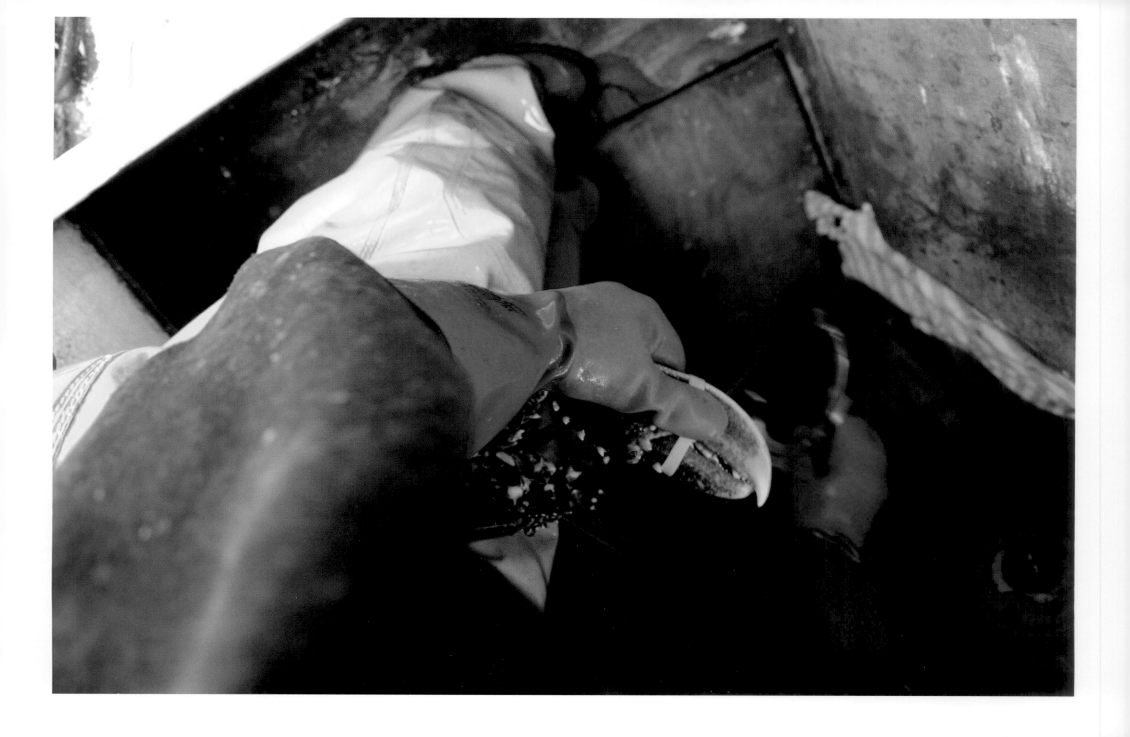

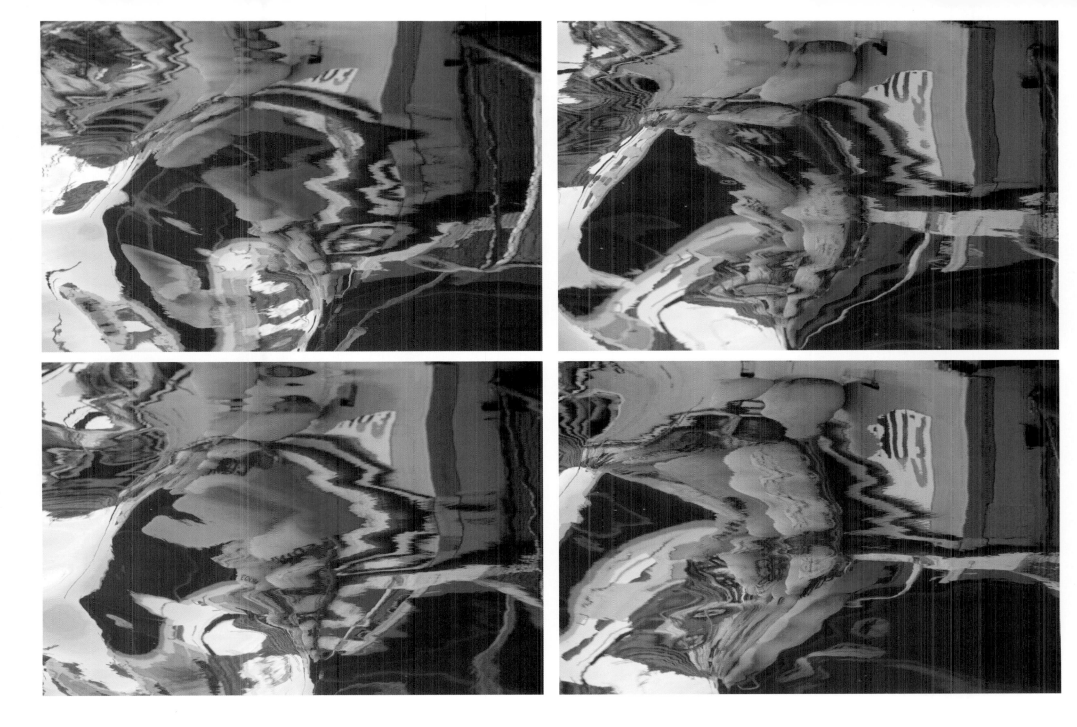

147

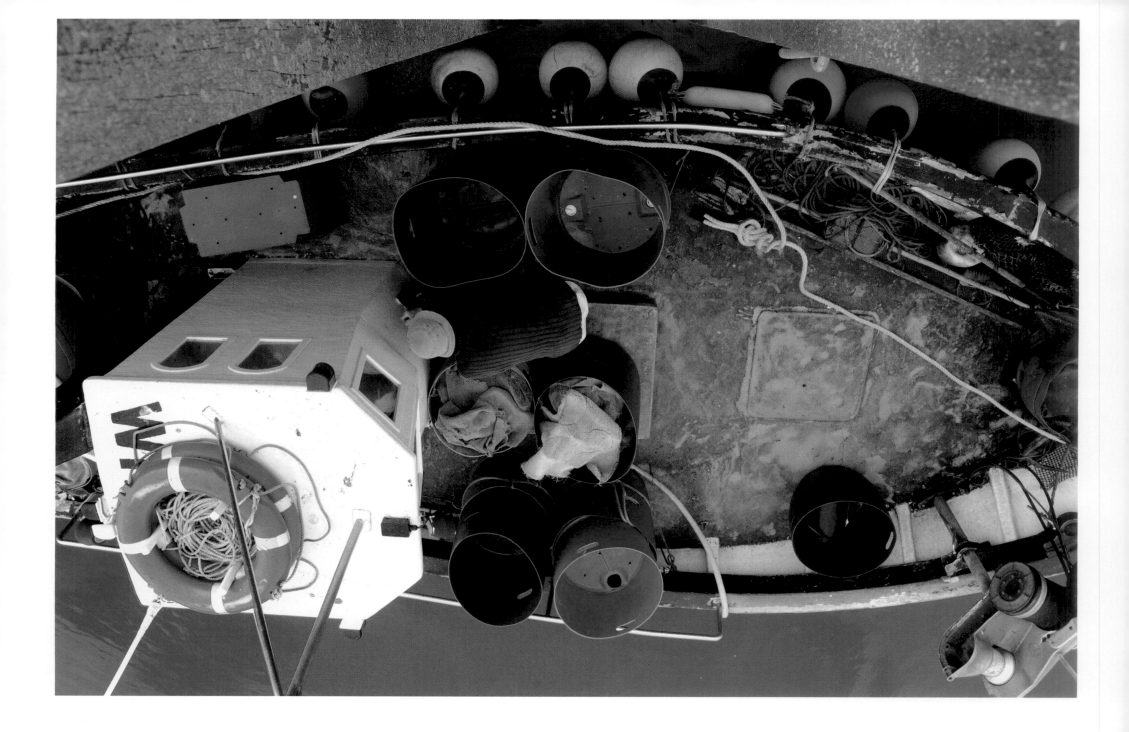

Ted Hook

Whelking, Crab and Lobster Potting

Ted Hook: I was 14, I reckon, when I started commercial fishing. I'm 29 now. I was always into fishing, with rods, when I was a kid and then when I was 13, 14, I started going out on the fishing boats, just chopping bait and stuff. At 16, I bought my first boat from money I earned working on the boats and winkle picking. I bought a license for the boat, did it up, it was a bit of a wreck and went whelk fishing in a place called Saundersfoot in West Wales. I went through three or four different boats there. It was good at first, but then the boom went there and so I came down here to West Bay when I was 20. I met my missus here.

There are not many rules and regulations for the kind of fishing I do, which is whelks, crabs and lobsters and it's a good close knit fishing community here. It's a nice harbour to get in and out of. You can just come and go as you please. To start off, I bought Jack's mooring and boat, Aquarius, off him when he gave up because of all the red tape. He was a sole fisherman but he couldn't make a living out of it anymore. Well, to make a living out of it, he would have had to have broken the law, which you shouldn't have to do. He was one of the few who actually owned his mooring. So that was a good investment. Because the whelk fishing off here is pretty good, you get quite a lot of visiting boats, so if I wanted to sell the mooring, I could sell it tomorrow for good money.

I've got a new boat now. It's safer and we've got more comfort. We've actually got seats in the wheelhouse. You get to have a cup of tea. We're about two hours faster a day when we're whelking, which is our main thing. It's also more stable. The other day, we had about 200 whelk pots on it. With the old boat, we wouldn't have dreamed of doing that.

You have to persist with fishing. When I first started, my friend's dad (who's boat I started on) said to me, "The one thing to do is just keep on with it. You'll get some real crap times and that's when most people give up. But keep on with it." And that's what I do. The start of this year was almost my lowest. I was almost at the point of giving up. "Fuck it, let's jack it in." My engine went bang, so I had no income for three months. If I had had to pay someone to mend my engine, I would have gone under, but I'm lucky I can do things myself. My colleague is good too. He's picked up a lot of stuff, like fibre-glassing. He's really good. The best crew I think I've ever had. I cannot fault the bloke. He's there all the time. He's like me. He just wants to work and earn money and keep himself to himself. That's what I want to do. I just want a peaceful life. I don't want the harbour politics and all that aggro. I just want to go to sea and go fishing. I just try and keep myself to myself and plod on.

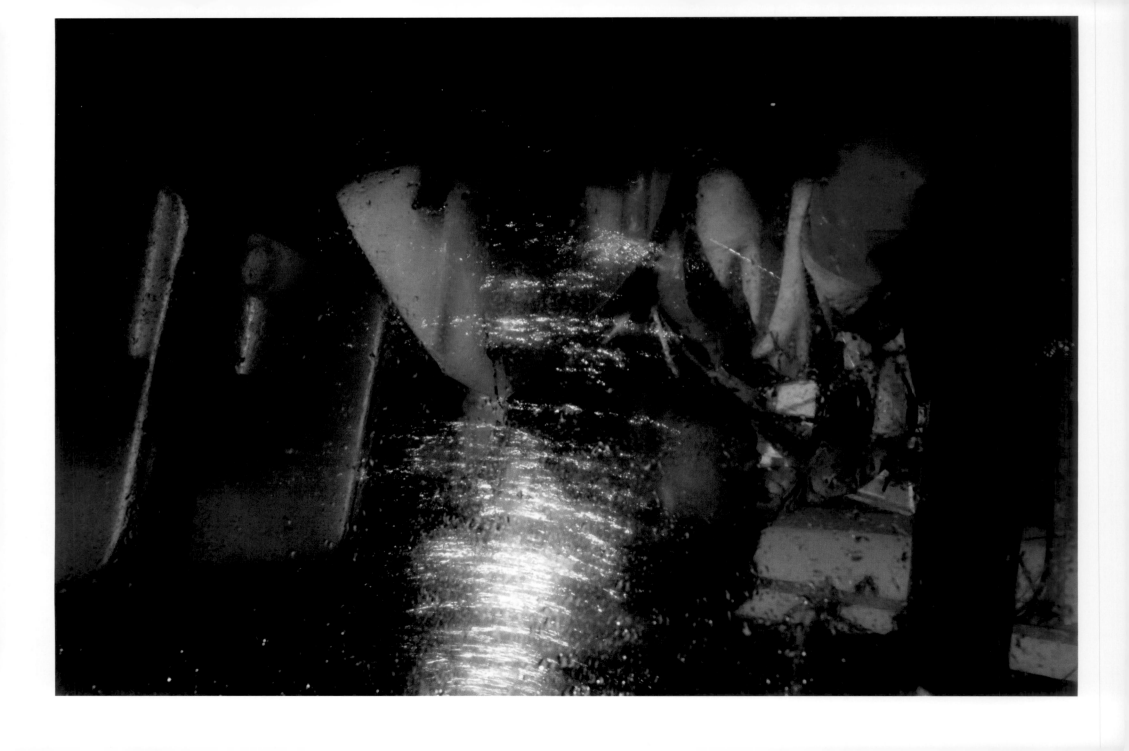

Jamie Smith

Netting

Jamie Smith: I've been fishing for 30 years in total, but turned it into a career 25 years ago. My current boat's been with me for nearly 20 years. It'll see me out. I'm not buying another one. It comes out of the water about every two years for a complete overhaul, usually during the winter. I do it all myself. I rebuilt the engine about eight years ago. It's done nearly 20,000 miles since then.

You really want to be able to carry out all your own maintenance and repairs to keep the costs down. It can be very expensive otherwise. You grow to like your boat. No boat is perfect, but you grow to know it. You become quite attached. I know fishermen who've retired and it's been the worst day of their lives when they've given up a boat that they've worked with for a long period of time. Really good boats are becoming harder and harder to find and they are horrendously expensive. To buy this boat, new, now would probably cost you in excess of £100,000. Then you've got to try to obtain the appropriate licenses. With licenses, my boat is probably worth something like £ 70-80,000, so it's quite a big investment.

Fishing is very important to my identity. You either love the sea or you don't. I look at the sea as my office space. Even though the rules and regulations get tighter, you've got a certain amount of freedom. When you go to sea, you leave everything else behind. If you like that kind of thing, then there's nothing else you can replace it with. It is as much of a lifestyle as it is for the money. If you work hard enough, then you'll earn a living on a boat of this size, but you'll never make a fortune. The only time you'll ever make any money, is the day you retire and sell the boat.

There's a certain camaraderie amongst the fishermen and with my customers, as I sell everything privately. The circle you get into is a bit of a social circle as well as a work circle. It becomes part of your life. I always feel, if I've missed a day at sea, I can't get that day back. It's probably one of the most unpredictable ways of earning a living there is. But at the same time, there's always a buzz; you always think you're going to have a better day tomorrow. All fishermen are hunters and at the end of the day, nobody can guarantee the fish to be there and even if it is there, you're not guaranteed to catch it. A lot of people haven't got that hunting instinct now but you quite often find fishing families have followed on, father and son for generations.

West Bay is quite a close-knit community. I think you'll find the same atmosphere in Lyme Regis and other small harbours. The biggest attraction in West Bay, as far as the tourists go, are the fishermen and the fishing. You've only got to put a box of fish on the quayside and there's a crowd there looking to see what you've caught. If they come from a city or something, it's a completely different way of life to them and they're often fascinated by it.

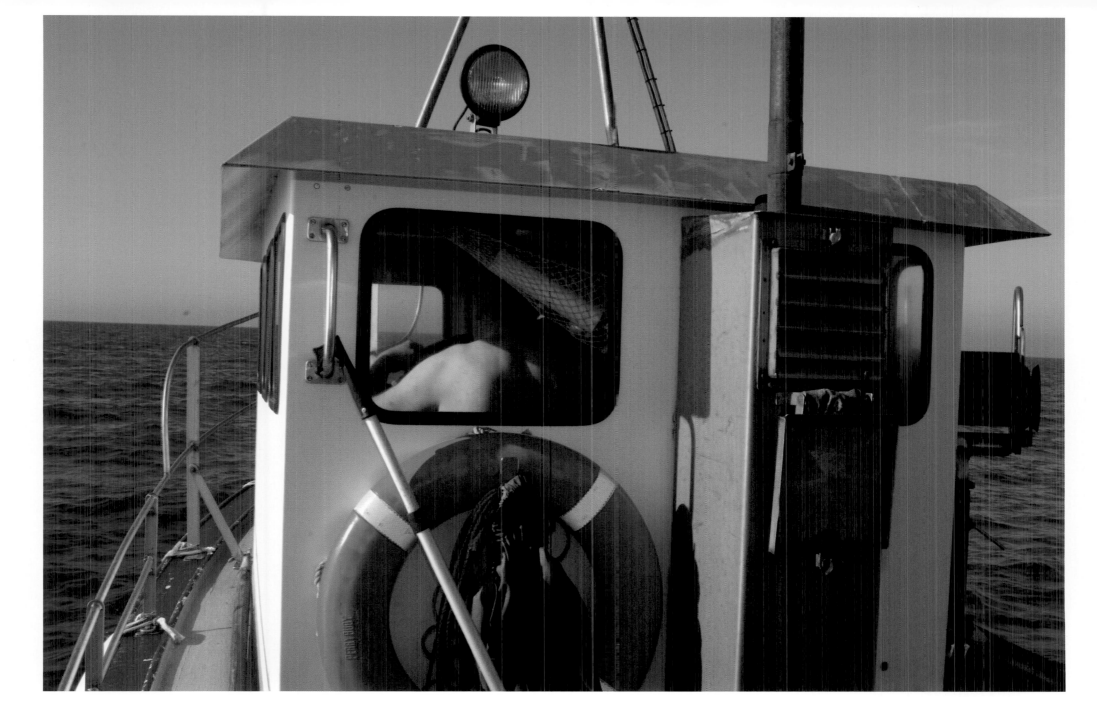

Aubrey Banfield

Netting, Cuttlefishing and Crab Potting

Aubrey Banfield: You can't beat being out here. You've got to be a sea lover obviously, but at the end of the day, everything's a surprise. I can have exceptional days or I can get nothing. But every day is a new day. It's not just the same old shit.

The icing on the cake, in terms of job satisfaction, is a good catch and it's also important for me to do what I want to do. I've spent the last 24 years, pretty much doing what I want, but not at the pace I want to do it at, because of the constraints of other people. With fishing, if I want to go out, I go. If I don't want to go out, I don't have to.

In the first three years of fishing, I didn't make a penny. After the first three years, and with the input, knowledge and help of the other fishermen, I started making money. It gets better every year. It's the same as any business venture. If you expect to make money in the first year, dream on. But I didn't go into it with my eyes shut, I knew it was going to be a hard slog.

The only thing that will stop me fishing is if I can't make it pay for itself. But I think it'll work and I'll keep going until retirement. I've always had a love of the sea. I'm living the dream. I'm going to work every day and I'm actually going fishing!

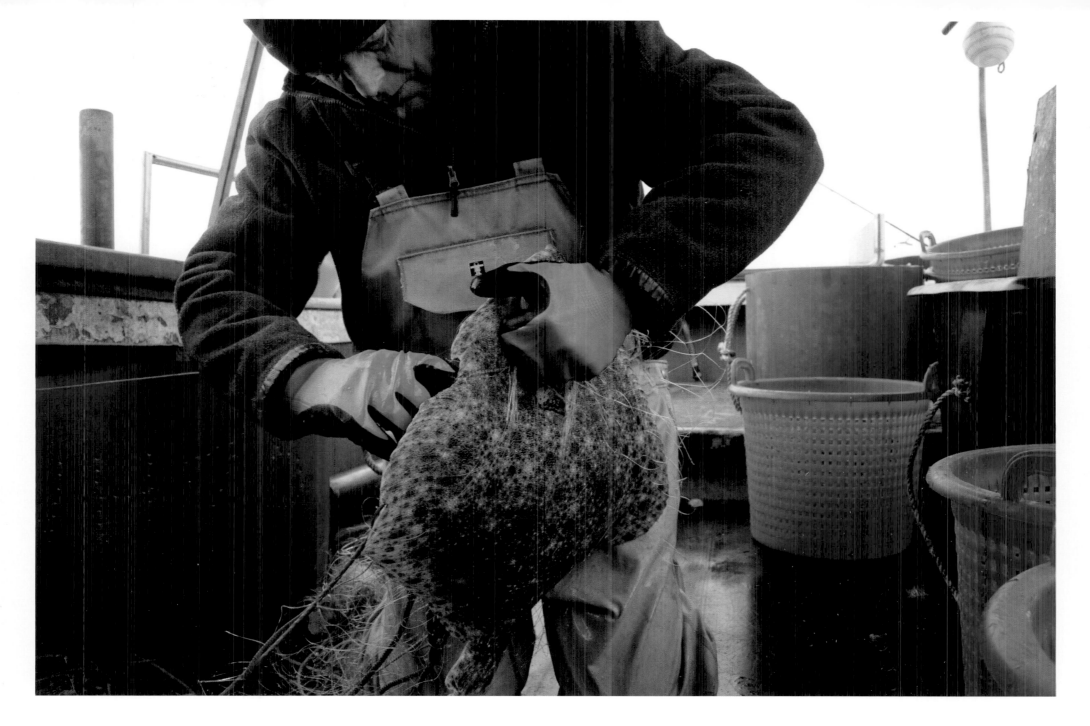

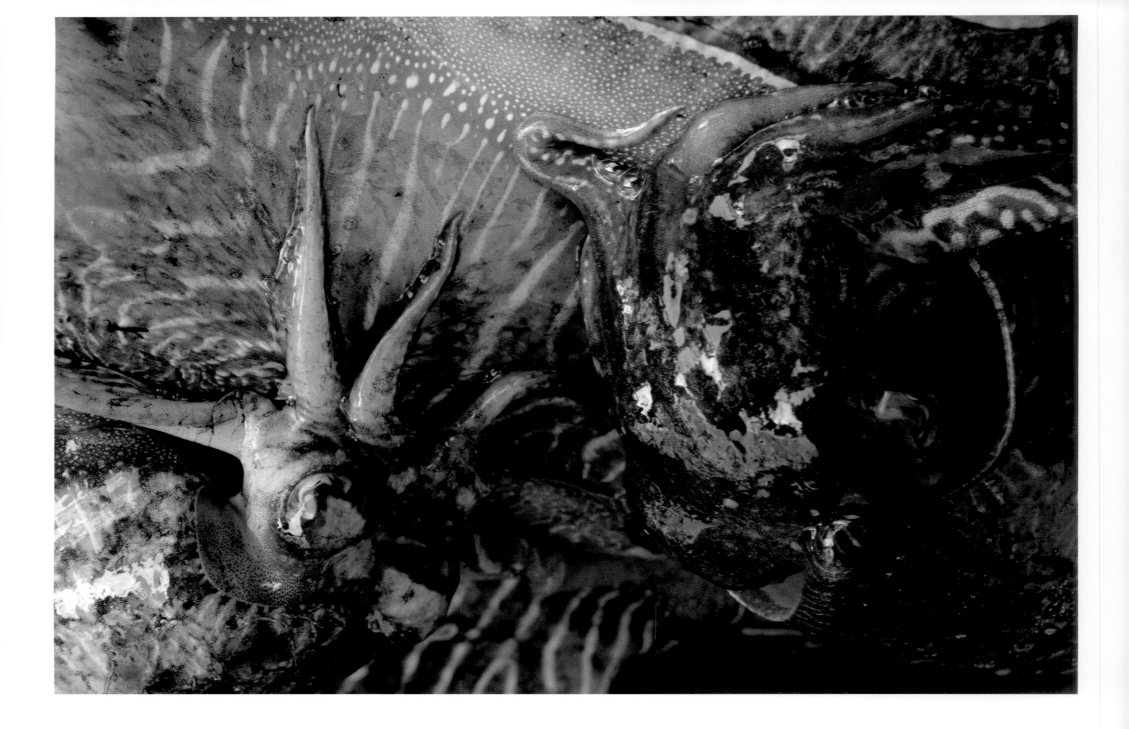

John Worswick

Scallop Diving

John Worswick: I've been diving for scallops since 1999. So about 18 years. I learnt to dive when I moved down here. I did a bit of diving with one of the other guys just for fun and thought, yep, I can find a few scallops. I'll give this a go. It's great when your living is your hobby and your hobby is your living! Can't be bad can it? It's pretty safe really, but complacency can be a recipe for disaster. If you're very meticulous with your gear, you make sure everything works before you jump in, then it's all going to be all right.

Probably the thing that's made the biggest difference to us here is that in 2007, 2008 we had had a marine protected area brought in which stopped trawling and dredging in a reasonably big area of Lyme Bay. Since then, the sea bed's recovered; the scallop stocks have recovered. It's all been pretty positive. I get more and bigger scallops because they're being left longer to grow.

We're a close community. I mean, we're all trying to earn a living, but it's in everybody's interest that we get on with each other and help each other out. One of the boats filled up with water and sunk recently. Nobody really knows what happened, but it went down in minutes. Fortunately the guys managed to get life jackets on and put out a distress call. It was Mark who heard them and notified the Coastguard.

I can't think what I'd do if I retired. I'd get bored stupid. I'd have to find something else to do, so if I can keep doing something I enjoy, and that pays me a few quid, it's got to be better than playing bowls. It's the hunter-gatherer thing I like. There aren't many jobs now where people are paid purely by their effort. Most people are paid by the week, by the month. Whereas every day, for us, the more you get, the more you earn. You've got an hour where nobody can get hold of you, there's no phone, nobody asking you anything, no noise. All you hear are bubbles and occasionally the boat when it comes to pick up a bag. But you are totally away from it.

I find it quite stress free, but I'm not sure everybody would! I don't find it hard work whatsoever but to some degree Jez does. He comes up with, "Oh I'm knackered!" whereas I don't. I think it's because he's been doing it three years and I've been doing it nearly 20. But I do find if I do some other form of exercise, I get knackered probably loads quicker. If I was fixing a car, laying under it, like Jez does, I'd struggle.

Stephen Elsworth

Crab and Lobster Potting

Stephen Elsworth: I was born and bred in Burton Bradstock, so I've been by the sea all my life. I started fishing from the beach with my Dad when I was four or five years old.

When I was about eight or nine, I was regularly lowered over the edge of the cliff by my brother, to collect seagull eggs. I would have a bit of rope round my waist but I never used to worry about the danger. We rarely ate the seagull eggs ourselves. We used to sell them. The cliffs were different then. They were covered in ledges about 18 inches apart. Now though, they're all smooth. I wouldn't do it now. No chance.

When I was 20, I started working on the trawlers. I gave it up, but still went out with Pete Newton during the holidays, on his boat. I learnt a lot from Pete.

I bought the boat that I've got now, 11 years ago. In the first year, I didn't have to do much to it, but in the second year I did, because it sank in the harbour. And that cost me a lot of money. Luckily, my in-laws helped me out, or I wouldn't still be fishing. When I first had the boat, I used to go out in all weathers. I sometimes used to think to myself, "What are you doing?! Why are you out here?!" because my boat's not the biggest. But nowadays, my wife says to me, "I'd rather you came home. What's the point of risking it just for a few quid?" I'll drive down to the Bay, look at the sea and if it's rough, I'll just go home.

I've got one company that takes every lobster I catch and all the medium and large crab. It all goes to the Hive café. To be honest, if it wasn't for them, I probably wouldn't still be fishing because they pay me well. They're all about local, sustainable fishing. I turn up there at 11 o'clock in the morning with a basket of fresh crab and all the holiday makers are like, "Ooo. Can we have a photo?" It's a great PR stunt isn't it! But, you know, I really enjoy it!

I think you have to be naturally savvy to be a fisherman. It's easy to spend a lot of money getting other people to do work on your boat. I do all the work myself; I do all the servicing. If I got someone else to do it, it would cost me 300 quid. I can do it myself for 70 pounds.

In this job, you have to have your wits about you all the time. You can't switch off. But I like to be on my own. I've got my own routine. I haven't got a wheelhouse full of electronics. I've got the basics and that's it. I don't see the point in having all these sonars. I've got a chartplotter which shows me where I am and that's all I need.

263

With enormous and heartfelt thanks to our sponsors, without whom this book would never have been printed

SML Marine Paints have been supplying the UK's fishermen and boat owners with quality paints since 2004. We pride ourselves in providing excellent customer service from the first time you speak to us. Every application can be different so we ensure we provide the best solution tailored to the protection you need, the time you have to complete the job and your budget.

When Damian first showed us the pictures of the Fishermen of Westbay we were amazed at how he has captured their day - we could almost taste the salty air and smell the ocean. We talk to boat owners and fishermen every day but rarely get to see our customers boats and how they use them. We wish Damian every success with Seabird and would like to say a big thank you to all our customers and the UK's brave and hard-working fishermen.

SML Marine Paints, The Downs, South Cerney, Cirencester. GL7 6DD. Telephone: 01285 862132. Email: info@smlpaints.co.uk Website: www.smlmarinepaints.co.uk

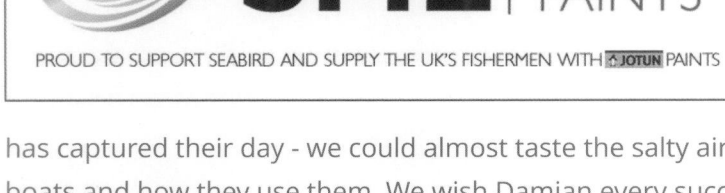

The Riverside Restaurant

The multi award winning Riverside Restaurant has been a feature of West Bay for over 50 years and is still providing some of the best cooked seafood in the area. Being staunch supporters of sustainable fishing and our local fisherman we are very proud to be supporting Seabird and wish Damian Bird every success. www.thefishrestaurant-westbay.co.uk

LEADING INNOVATION
Cheetah Marine is a long established family run business with a very practical approach.
www.cheetahmarine.co.uk

Now approaching its 30th year, O'Three Ltd has grown into an international brand renowned for its high end niche range of neoprene dry suits, wet suits, accessories and incredible detail for customer service. O'Three is passionate about the sea and is proud to have helped support Damian Bird with bring SEABIRD to print.
O'Three Ltd | Osprey Quay | Portland | Dorset | DT5 1BL | www.othree.co.uk | 01305 822820

COASTALNETS
The UK's leading supplier of nets for ANY application

Coastal Nets have proudly supported the fishing fleet for over 30 Years. Please visit our website for a comprehensive list of our commercial fishing equipment.
www.coastalnets.co.uk

A long established provider of marine insurances for fishing vessels and workboats.
www.arnottmarine.co.uk

Groves Nurseries is Bridport's award-winning family run garden centre. Through six generations they have been growing plants in West Dorset since 1866. Their Bridport garden centre has everything you need for the garden, a pet shop and a restaurant.
Go to www.grovesnurseries.co.uk for more information.

More than just fish and chips. Longs is a family run business that has two locations, where you can eat in at our restaurants or outside tables or take away traditional fish and chip shop fare, we also make a varied specials menu that changes regularly.
15 King Street and 23 West street, Bridport.
www.longsbridport.co.uk

Washingpool Farm is run by three generations of the Eveleigh/Holland family.
Est. in 1971 the business has grown dramatically to now include an award winning farm shop, restaurant, fishing lakes, CL caravan site & two lovely holiday cottages. All situated on a 30 acre working farm that produces its own Devon Ruby Red beef, lamb, pork, eggs and a vast array of fruit, vegetables, flowers and potatoes. www.washingpool.co.uk

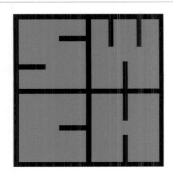

South West Crane Hire, your local, long established, family run crane hire company.
Look to us for a quick, reliable and safe solution to your lifting needs.
www.swch.co.uk

Imex International is a family run business, established more than 35 years who provide high quality live shellfish, sourced directly from fishermen in the UK and surrounding waters, delivering throughout Europe with their own fleet of Vivier lorries.

Please contact Miguel Rivera on Tel 01423 868000, Mob 07801 695002

or email miguel@imex-international.co.uk   www.imex-international.co.uk

Award winning baker.

www.thecornishbakery.com

Darch Oil. 35 Oxford Rd, Pen Mill Trading Estate, Yeovil, Somerset. BA21 5HR

01935 473 302

www.darchoil.com

Davy's Locker is committed to the under 10 metre fleet in West Bay, believes in sustainable fishing and is proud to sell their catch.

www.davyslocker.co.uk

Echomaster Marine Ltd are one of the UK's leading supplier and Distributor of Marine Electronics products and Services. Whether buying from one of our approved Dealers around the UK, or directly; you can be assured of a professional level of Sales , Installation and Technical Support at all times. We take great care and pride to ensure we continue to meet your expectations and have one of the best customer reputations in the industry.

Visit our website www.echomastermarine.co.uk , or call us directly on 01261 831644 to discuss your next Electronics project or purchase.

...around since 1999. Today we service many industries but started very small, working with pot fishermen, designing, manufacturing and sourcing the materials they needed to improve their gear. We have been keen to promote conservation in pot fishing, making V notchers, escape rectangles and inexpensive size gauges. We still do this but we have expanded to include USA techniques of trap making, adapting them for our species and providing successful alternatives to traditional pot construction.
www.gtproductsmarine.com

Harbour News
West Bay, Bridport DT6 4EN.
Phone: 01308 423828

Sicor International are worldwide manufacturers & suppliers of nets, ropes & twines for fishing, marine & shipping, sports, leisure, agriculture and many industrial applications please see our website for information www.sicor-int.com

THE STATION KITCHEN BY

Located in West Bay, the fabulous Station Kitchen restaurant offers high-end dining, in their vintage 1911 train carriage. The carriage was used during WWI as a makeshift hospital carriage, it was used to transport injured British troops back from the Battle of the Somme, no less.
https://www.station.kitchen/

Beach & Barnicott

6 South Street, Bridport, Dorset.
Tel: 01308 425671
www.beachandbarnicott.co.uk

A company you can warm to.
www.southernfuels.co.uk

Engineering and bespoke fabrication services for local businesses and the general public.

West Country Catch supplies quality fresh fish to restaurants in and around Dorset, Devon and Somerset, we are based in Weymouth a seaside town in Dorset. We source our quality fish from Weymouth and Portland boats as well as from Brixham, Plymouth and Newlyn day boats, we are in constant contact with local fisherman as well as our buyers in Brixham and Cornwall throughout day, which keeps us up to date with what is due to be landed enabling us to provide our customers with some of the finest fish off the coast of Dorset, Devon and Cornwall. www.westcountrycatch.com Tel: 01305 259135.

7 St Andrews Industrial Estate
Bridport
Dorset. DT6 3EX
01308 456232 www.seawinch.com

No.10
Cafe | Bar

Bridport - Dorset

10 East St, Bridport DT6 3LF
Phone: 01308 420032
Find us on Facebook

www.britishamericanchamberofcommerce.com

West Bay Tea Rooms
Truly Scrumptious Homemade Cakes & Light Lunches

West Bay Tea Rooms, 2 Maritime House, West Bay, DT6 4GD.
info@westbaytearooms.co.uk, www.westbaytearooms.co.uk

West Bay Tea Rooms is the ideal place to relax and refuel, what's more we're perfectly situated to explore West Bay and the beautiful Jurassic coast. We pride ourselves on our freshly prepared, locally sourced and homemade food and celebrate 'the cup of tea' with over 40 different blends to choose from! Plus with a delicious selection of cakes, homemade scones, light lunches and daily specials there's something for everyone.
Tel: 01308 455697

www.mobilemarine.uk.com
mobilemarine@btconnect.com
01297 631821 / 07798 683572

"Congratulations! Very nice!"
Ami Vitale. American photojournalist
Nikon Ambassador
and National Geographic photographer

"Congratulations, this is awesome!!"
David James.
Steven Spielberg and Tom Cruise's
specialist film-stills photographer.

LIFE FORCE

"This looks absolutely beautiful! ...and a huge congrats!"
Catherine Karnow.
National Geographic photographer

"You can almost smell the ocean and hear the gulls as Damian Bird provides up close images and personal stories of Britain's coastal fishermen."
Robert Young-Pelton.
Canadian-American author, journalist
and documentary filmmaker.